PRINCIPLES

OF

THE REVOLUTION:

SHOWING THE PERVERSION OF THEM AND THE CONSEQUENT FAILURE OF THEIR ACCOMPLISHMENT.

BY J. P. BLANCHARD.

BOSTON:
PRESS OF DAMRELL AND MOORE,
16 DEVONSHIRE STREET.
1855.

PRINCIPLES OF THE REVOLUTION.

THE American Revolution is yet unaccomplished, or it is a splendid failure. It rose before the world on a basis of political purity, undiscerned in the speculations of heathen philosophy, or the vaunted intelligence of European civilization. The development of the truth, that all men have equal right to life, to liberty, and the pursuit of happiness, broke on the anxious sight of millions of the oppressed, as the harbinger of their release from the thraldom of ages. We have come upon the day when the mournful disappointment of all these hopes is no longer doubtful. The despots of Europe, and the military chiefs of South America, still wave their sceptres of steel over the most enlightened portions of the globe; and when their struggling vassals turn their eyes to our self-gratulating Republic, they hear not amid the rattling chains of slavery, see not through the smoke of our martial desolations, feel not in the nets of our monopolizing legislation, and the cramps of our antiquated jurisprudence, the liberty and safety their ardent desires anticipated. Our land is yet sought by the starving for food, by the impoverished for remunerated labor; but the El Dorado dream of freedom, prosperity, and equal rights, has vanished with the awakening of the age. The unseen leaders of conflicting parties now hold in their grasp the potent ballot-box, from which popular government was unwisely expected: departed patriotism has left its name and its cloak to cover avidity for the spoils of office: republican economy has given place to excessive indirect taxation, and profuse, ostentatious expenditure. Our professions of peace and forbearance are falsified by our martial spirit and rapacious hostile encroachments.

And in all this there is no degeneracy. On the contrary, as a people, in our individual and social relations, we are improved. Since our Revolution, religion, literature, science, have spread over our land their healing wings: extending commerce has bound us to our race in a humanizing chain of brotherhood, and the new-born spirit of reform, searching through the dark caverns of moral corruption, is bringing their hideous forms of evil into day, and preparing to light up the flame of charity with their consuming remains. Those who look back to the birth of our nation, as the Saturnian age of purity, cherish a misdirecting illusion. Our revolutionary fathers saw but obscurely the forms of the liberty and justice their language proclaimed. It is true, the Declaration of Independence held "these truths to be self-evident; that, all men are created equal; that they are endowed by their Creator with certain inalienable rights; that among these are life, liberty, and the pursuit of happiness"; but the Constitutions professed to be formed on the basis of this declaration, and still more the laws and actual practice under them, exhibit but little departure from the usages of the mother land. There is still the same unlimited power in the States—so far as not granted to the Union—to regulate every commercial and social relation in private life; still the same authority in the voluminous and perplexing decisions of courts; the same predominance given to the domination of government, or the majority of the people, over the interests and rights of individuals; still the same oppressive power in judicial officers; the same exclusive reliance on physical force, and the menace of personal or pecuniary punishment for the maintenance of order, and still the same compulsion to civil and military service; and these ungranted usurpations were deliberately re-enacted by our patriot fathers, in the face of their "self-evident truths," with strangely inconsistent blindness. These "self-evident truths" were never understood, and the experiment of political liberty and equal rights, so loudly announced, has never yet been made.

The source of this unhappy delusion, which still clouds the minds of our greatest statesmen, is not difficult to discover.

The interpretation of the self-evident truths proclaimed, was drawn from a heathen, and not from a Christian criterion: the authority of Christianity is scarcely recognized in our Constitutions, and was perhaps but little contemplated by the framers: the only revelation of principles by which the oppressive corruptions of the world can be dissolved, was utterly disregarded. An infusion of some of the ordinances of Judaism, repealed by Christ, was indeed mingled with the laws of some of the States; but when our revolutionary patriots felt the injustice of the feudal maxims, under which they suffered, and desired to throw off these venerated oppressions from their shoulders, they looked back to the fascinating republics of Greece and Rome, for guidance to the security of their asserted rights. This delusion still continues; it pervades the public mind; for it is fostered by the influence of our leading statesmen, brought up under the dazzling impressions of classical tuition.

But these ancient republics had no true conception of political liberty; their ideas of it were only the abrogation of all prerogative from birth or fortune, and the participation of the people at large in the creation and maintenance of government. The reservation of independent right to the citizen; the exemption of the individual from all unnecessary rule of the community—the only conditions of true political freedom—were never dreamed of. The dignity of man, as such, and the comforts of domestic and social relations, were alike sacrificed to public policy: patriotism was the paramount virtue; and the grandeur of the State was upheld by the submersion of the interests of humanity. That men were created "equal," was perceived; but not that they had "inalienable rights." No! they were closely cemented portions of the republican temple; passive particles of the popular vortex which carried them unresistingly along. Plain is the misnomer to call this "liberty:" the avowed despotism of hereditary sovereigns can never be more rigorous, more irresponsible, more irresistible, than the overwhelming tyranny of ephemeral chiefs, sustained by an admiring and deluded majority. Surely the truth of this proposition can no longer be disputed in this our self-lauded time and country: we have mournful experience of this calamity; and yet its demonstrable origin is hidden from our eyes. We yet believe that the institutions of our revolutionary fathers were the *ne plus ultra* of wisdom ; and the evils inevitably consequent upon them, which we endure, are but temporary perversions.

That all men are created equal, and endowed with inalienable rights, are not self-evident propositions, for they have been ignored in all ages ; and are yet unacknowledged by the greater part of mankind. In their true legitimate sense, they are yet discerned but by few. Our fathers came to them by a reasoning forced upon them by the circumstances of their case. Smarting under wrongs imposed upon them by the combined aristocracy and hierarchy of the parent land, they sought a general principle, which should obliterate permanent political distinctions, founded on birth, rank, or affluence ; and by the language in which they declared this principle, they probably intended no more than an assertion of the innate equality of all political right among men ; and this coinciding with the sentiments of the republics of antiquity, the institutions they formed were founded upon their example. They were however providentially led to a language, which truly comprises a deeper, juster, and more felicitous import ; providentially, for the keen reforming spirit of the advancing age, discovering the unforeseen conformity of these alleged political axioms with the principles of the Gospel, will make them the basis of a peaceful revolution, far more radical and beneficent than that of our revolutionary patriots ; which shall throw off the heavier incubus they deemed essential to government, as they threw off the lighter one imposed by the throne of Britain.

Had our patriot fathers gathered the truths they called "self-evident," from the pages of the New Testament, interpreted them by the instructions of Christ, and cherished them in his spirit, the Constitutions they would have formed upon them would have been much more worthy of our reverence and obedience. The accumulated corruptions of tyrannical ages would have been shatterred to fragments, in the explosion they made of the divine right of kings, priests and nobles. This error was again providential, for the measure would have been premature; the age was not prepared for it. To have caused a political fabric to emerge at once from a chaos of prescriptive impositions, cleansed from their stains and imbued with Christian justice, would have been an achievement too vast for human wisdom; and its purity would have been invisible to eyes not yet awakened from the torpor of servitude. The time has perhaps now arrived when the true principles of Christian policy should be laid open to the eyes of our countrymen.

Political government is a necessary evil. That it is an evil, will be acknowledged by every clear-sighted philanthropist; that it is a necessity, will be held by every statesman, who, contemplating the selfish and disorderly passions of many men, sees in it the only refuge from violence, injury and wrong. That it has ever fully accomplished this, its professed object, will hardly be asserted by any intelligent observer. In view of its universal oppressions, such a one would not go far beyond the truth who should assert that in every nation it has only transferred the injury and wrong from individual to governmental action; for protection is everywhere given at the cost of liberty, and often of right. Eminent politicians hold that partial abrogation of human freedom is demanded for human safety; but a far greater part is usually taken than is requisite for this purpose; and this is ever inadequate, as the most vigorous governments do not succeed in suppressing all the evils they are constituted to remedy.

But in truth, even this principle is not sincerely acted upon. In the formation of governments, the strength of the government, and not the safety of the citizen, has been the invariable object of solicitude. It is true that in our several Constitutions, provisions are made to protect individuals from illegal exercise of power, in the administrators of the government, but none whatever to shield them from the tyranny of the laws themselves; and scarcely any to avert the oppression of a barbarous jurisdiction, originally formed to sustain the prerogatives of sovereigns, never assented to by the people, and yet having all the force of law. The legislation and jurisdiction of the United States are indeed expressly limited, but those of the States are only restricted by the grant to the general government; no reservation of political power is made in either to individual citizens.

Obvious and undeniable as is this fact, still the cry by which we delude ourselves and impose on foreign nations, is, that ours is a government of the people; is sustained, regulated, and may be changed by the people; and it is intended to be understood, that this "people" is a majority of persons in the nation acting as individuals, but in concert and uniformity. The circumstance is overlooked, that with the diversity of human sentiments, no such accordance is possible; and no laws could be made by any such supposed concert, on unexpected subjects of a legislation, which is not permitted to the people; for they are only allowed to elect by vote the persons who are to frame and execute the laws. Even in the exercise of this power they are not free; for, as if every citizen voted for the true representative of his opinions, no majority could be found, and consequently no laws enacted; every citizen is under the necessity of voting for the nominee of his party leaders, whether preferred or not, for the sake of union. Except in some test issue of opposing parties, the voter cannot know the opinion of his candidate, on many of the objects for which he will be called to legislate; nor can these representatives know the views of but a small portion of their constituents, on the laws they enact. It is probable that many of the laws made by Congress would not meet the full concurrence of but a small part of the people throughout the country, if their opinions could be separately and privately ascertained. It is a glaring fallacy to call this a self-government of the people by representation.

If, however, our government were truly one of a majority of the people by representation, it would still have failed to give security to the individual rights prefacing the Declaration of Independence; for the legislation of the majority thus supposed to be represented, has no limits imposed upon it in favor of individual rights, or those of the minority who may dissent from such legislation, in any measures they may deem it expedient to enact. The democratic theory is that the majority of voters must have all rule; and when we consider that in all republican countries this majority is necessarily led by a few, we perceive that this democratic maxim is as fatal to individual freedom, as the autocracy of a despot. The common notion that a majority may be safely trusted not to make or permit any laws to oppress themselves as individuals, supposes a higher degree of popular intelligence and individual independence than anywhere exists;

and the history of all countries, and none more than our own, fully disproves the fact.

Another consideration showing the failure of our republican institutions to secure the rights declared in our Declaration of Independence, is, that whatever may be the influence of the popular mind in shaping the laws made by its supposed representatives, these laws do in fact form but a minor part of the authority by which the people are governed. The action of legislation comes, for the most part, but indirectly and remotely on the people. Executive power indeed presses upon them, in conformity to the laws; but only on extraordinary occasions; and sometimes with a severity which the laws do not contemplate. In the regulation of individual concerns, which government has usurped, and wherever private rights are invaded, the decision of all questions and the enforcement of all law rests with the judiciary. This is the power which comes in perpetual contact with the people, and which constitutes almost the whole of the government to them. But this branch of the government has never been revolutionized. No provision was made by our fathers to limit judicial action to the Constitutions and laws; and voluminous and perplexing as these laws often are—as they cover but a small part of the judicial maxims considered as "settled,"—in far the greater proportion of cases, individual rights are determined and protected by what is termed "common law"—on which there is no legislation. If this common law is understood to mean a rational sense of justice in every intelligent mind, no better authority could be adduced for every private judgment; but unhappily no other common law is discernible by our judges, than the decisions established in the kingdom from which we seceded, which being overruled or influenced by regal authority, and designed chiefly for the security of governmental power, are but little suited to the principles on which our Revolution proceeded. We indeed exult in Magna Charta, and the trial by jury, called the bulwarks of British liberty; but whatever advance of freedom these regulations may be on former royal supremacy, examination will show them to be as far behind the principles of our Revolution. While therefore we boast of popular self-government, we are yet for the greatest part of that government, still under the dominion of a foreign sovereignty, which we have abjured and denounced.

In speaking of the in adequacy of the trial by jury to protect individual rights, it must be understood that reference is made to the jury of practice, and not the jury of theory. Were there indeed a real trial by jury, in which twelve unbiased men should decide any case according to their sense of natural justice, in disregard of all law, precedent or authority, such a tribnnal would be more conformed to the principles of our Revolution, than any judicial regulation ever yet made by nations. The perplexing and delusive study of law might be, in a great measure, forborne, and simplicity, uniformity and justice be the result. As no decision would be a guide for another, any error of judgment would affect but one case only, and would not be perpetuated. As the practice is, we have been hardly benefited by the change from being a king-ridden to being a judge-ridden people.

If the principles of the Revolution have thus failed of practical results, in those parts of the Union where their operation is least restricted, and where they are most in unison with the spirit and habits of the people, how much more complete is their failure in those States, where, by the prevalence of slavery, they are utterly obliterated! In the domination of a comparatively few slaveholders over ten times as many slaves, and in their imperative influence over as great a number of nominally freemen, who, by their poverty and ignorance, are brought into entire sympathy with the slavemasters, we behold an aristocracy of the most oppressive and debasing nature, in which no trace is discernible of the equal rights of men, which their progenitors, as well as ours, proclaimed to the world; and when we reflect that this aristocratic state of society has not only thus overwhelmed every principle of revolutionary freedom within its own pale, but, by political corruptions, has been enabled to extend its awful pall over other States yet exempt from that tyrannical institution, we perceive at once that our vaunting declaration of the equal rights of man to "life, liberty, and the pursuit of happiness," has as yet found no practical establishment in this Western empire.

But there is another circumstance which appears to close this question. The framers of our government, in their solicitude for legislative independence, not only overlooked the tyrannical tendency of judicial powers, but the still greater imcompatibility with liberty, of military establishments. Having gained their independence by the supposed necessity of martial operations; having before them the example, not only of the States of antiquity, but of every modern community revolutionized into some semblance of republicanism by force of arms; and alarmed at the disorganizing developments of a new-formed, unsettled nation, it was natural that they should seek to provide for national defence and order by a vast military organization. It is true, that, in recollection of cases in which nominal Commonwealths have been overthrown by military dictators, they feared the establishment of a large standing army, and considered the liberties of the country more safe under the protection of a general militia force — a feeling which yet prevails in the country; but the danger is directly the reverse. In an intelligent, vigorous, and widely-dispersed nation, sensitively jealous of their imagined freedom, there need be little fear that any commander or any army, however powerful, would be able to overthrow their political institutions by open force. The only opportunity conceivable for this purpose was in the case of Washington, after the Revolution, who was too patriotic to avail himself of it; and it is not likely any other man will ever arise in this land of conflicting parties so generally popular as to attempt it with success. The government of Great Britain maintains a large standing army, which in time of peace is principally employed as a police force; yet no Englishman has the least anxiety lest the organization of his government should be changed by military power: the late popular Duke of Wellington would have attempted it in vain.

The true nature of a military despotism does not consist in the mere presence of a military force, however powerful, but in the principles on which that force is employed: these are two — the supposed necessity of preserving order and protecting rights by force, and the supposed moral obligation of obedience to commanders, without any regard to the righteousness of the command. Any citizen cherishing these principles as truths, is already a willing slave to military tyranny, and may be made an instrument of it whenever called on by his rulers for that service. When therefore these principles are confined to the officers and soldiers of a standing army, there is little danger from them to the rest of the people, as these forces are restrained from injury to them by the strictness of military discipline; but when — as by a general militia system — these principles are diffused through the whole community, every citizen becomes a tyrant over his brother citizen, when so enjoined by the caprices of his government; and the greatest evil of military despotism — mental slavery — is universally established. The proposition that free citizens may be relied on never to submit to political subjection, or to impose it upon others, is overborne by the imagined obligation of obedience in military service.

These views are not merely hypothetical. In many instances, where portions of the militia have been called out to suppress tumults of the people, they have come with reluctance, and under a delusive sense of duty: in the most of such cases, the people have been right, and the government wrong; and in almost all, the injury inflicted by the military on the rights of citizens — even sometimes to the destruction of life — has been much greater than could reasonably have been expected from the unrestrained violence of the gatherings they quelled. It may be safely laid down as a maxim, that whenever a mob is too strong to be suppressed by a numerous and well-organized civil police, the object of that mob is such as ought not to be put down: it is the natural and never-yielded right of opposing governmental crime.

But it is said that the prevalence of these views would disorganize society; would destroy all government; lead to universal anarchy; expose all rights to violation, or protect them only by Lynch law. Such language is common in the mouths of our statesmen and judges, and given forth as self-evident propositions. They are not, however, self-evident; and, as far as we know, no shadow of proof of them has ever been attempted. They must go upon the assumption that the greatest part of the community are rogues and robbers, and are only restrained by the strong arm of law from general rapine. But if this were the case, no government could exist here but an absolute monarchy, supported by a standing force. The criminals of a community should undoubtedly be restrained; but they are, in every country, and we certainly hope in ours, but a small portion of the people, and may easily be checked, as far as is now done, by the ordinary civil police of the government. No instance can be produced of any great combination, having in view the abrogation of the government itself by force, or the destruction of the rights professed to be protected by it. Whatever forbearance may be shown to illegal combinations, the laws against single criminals — the only rightful object of government — would remain as strong as ever.

Although the mass of our citizens are blind to this condition of their country, intelligent men see and confess it; yet even with these, the language of justification is, "How can it be avoided? Where is the use of pointing out evils that are irremediable? All human institutions are necessarily imperfect; and the most that can be done, is to bring them as near to perfection as possible: this has been done in the formation of our government: it is the best that wisdom has ever yet devised; and certainly secures to us a greater measure of freedom and justice than any yet known in the world. Whatever may be the rigor of the laws on overt acts, we have still left to us the freedom of religious worship, of speech, writing, the press, popular assemblies, and social intercourse, untouched by the hand of government, and enjoyed to a greater extent than in any other land. Any change would probably be for the worse. Why not be contented with it as it is?" These representations, often made, are but partially true. Although our government usually refrains from violation of the rights enumerated, yet in many cases it fails to protect them; and in many instances, gives power to tyrannical individuals, who make these violations. The argument partly confesses, and partly denies, the proposition we maintain, that the principles of the Revolution have not been realized. It is remarkable that the rights here spoken of as unassailed, are enjoyed as fully (and even more so,) in the kingdom from which we separated, as with us; and therefore, did not spring from the Revolution, nor do they come up to its principles: they are held sacred by governments which openly deny the equal rights of man, and practically restrain the physical freedom and pursuit of happiness in their subjects.

The usual assertion that all governments—ours included—are imperfect, is an admission of a partial failure of the attempt to establish our revolutionary rights. The difference here maintained is, that this failure is complete : but when it is inferred, that because of this necessary imperfection, and because our government is in advance of all others yet constructed, no attempt should be made to bring it nearer to conformity with its theoretic principles, an argument is employed, which the intelligent men who use it would be ashamed to offer on any other subject than politics. If a merchant should enter a new business, on a new scheme, which promised more profit than others ; and should find after some years of trial that he failed to make these profits ; and should perceive that this failure was owing to mismanagement in departing from his original plan, we think he would hardly conclude to continue the business in the same faulty manner, for fear of a loss in reforming it.

The necessary imperfection of human government is readily acknowledged, and no expectation is entertained that the principles of the Revolution can ever be entirely and effectually carried out ; but that they may be so to every desirable extent, and may promote the liberty, justice and prosperity of the people to a degree never yet attained, is not disproved by the failure of our government to fulfil that purpose. The truth is, that the experiment has never yet been tried. The "self-evident" truths announced in the Declaration of Independence, and Bills of Rights of several States, that all men are created equal, endowed with the "inalienable" rights of "life, liberty, and the pursuit of happiness," were ignored in the very original construction of our several governments, which, with some improvements, were wholly founded on the basis of the principles of power maintained by the corrupt governments of other nations. In the Declaration, indeed, these rights are subjected to power in the very sentence in which they are declared ; for while in the first part, they are asserted to be the endowment of the Creator, and pronounced "inalienable," in the immediate sequel it is said that governments derive their power to secure (of course to control,) them "from the consent of the governed." Now as this consent is impossible, and never was, nor ever can be given, the power assumed to regulate these rights is consequently a usurpation, without any just authority. It is plain, that whenever government assumes to secure any right of one man by power, it must be by the restriction of the natural right of some other man; and this power has not its origin in the consent of the one thus restricted; but simply in the necessity of justice which disregards all abstract rights.

We know that this conclusion has been attempted to be evaded by the allegation, that the resignation of part of the natural rights of the individual is made in the formation of a Constitution or Government by compact. The legal maxim, that the ancestor may bind his successors as well as himself, in regard to property, is most irrationally extended to moral obligation; and it is accordingly held, that the compromises made by the framers of the National and State Constitutions, are obligatory on the consciences of all citizens now living under them. Thus, it is said, in the Preamble of the Constitution of Massachusetts — "The body politic is formed by a voluntary association of individuals: it is a social compact, by which the whole people covenants with each citizen, and each citizen with the whole people, that all shall be governed by certain laws for the common good." A sufficient reply to this would be, that, in point of fact, no such compact was ever made, either in Massachusetts or in any other country; and if it is said, that if not personally by the people themselves, it was by their representatives, — the plain answers are, that but a small part of the people were ever represented; that many citizens expressly dissented from the Constitution; and that such defect of representation or dissent, even by the smallest minority, invalidates the whole contract, as a general one; and that it therefore binds only those who expressly agreed with their enacting representatives.

But we are aware, that they are not facts, but presumptions, that are made the basis of political institutions; and it is gravely held, that, although no such compact as is supposed was made in reality, it is presumed to have been made, as no other foundation can be found for the existing "body politic." Admitting for a moment, that the presumption of a fact shall stand as good for a premise, as the fact itself, it must be one which is possible or conceivable: an absurdity cannot be premised. It is easy to show, that the alleged compact in question is not only an impossible, but even an inconceivable case. A compact is an agreement between two or more parties, by which one party confers on another a right affecting itself, which that other did not previously possess; and for such a grant, there must be at least two parties: there can be no compact of one party only. Now in the supposed compact by which government is formed, there are not two, but only one party. When it said, that "the whole people covenants with each citizen, and each citizen with the whole," we ask, Who is this "whole?" We understand the whole, in this case, to be an imagined aggregation of every citizen; and if each citizen gives assent together, they become a whole; and it is clearly a whole contracting with itself. If we say that each citizen gives his consent only as an individual, then where is the consenting whole, with whom he contracts? Does the citizen contract as one of the whole, and as an individual at the same time? Then again the two supposed parties are united in the same persons, who transfer no right to any other. Shall we set aside the nonentity, here called "the whole," and say that each individual citizen contracts with each other individual separately? then the contract is plainly made only by those who become express parties to it, and binds no other individual living at the same time; and not a single person who should afterwards be born; which would exempt almost all the the present inhabitants of Massachusetts, who have not sworn to support the Constitution on entering office. The presumption of a compact of each and all the citizens is therefore an inconceivable idea.

It is said, however, that this principle of compact standing at the head of the Constitution of Massachusetts, as its basis, every person who remains in its territory, submits to its laws, and avails himself of its protection, thereby gives assent to the government; and if he dislikes it, he is at liberty to retire from political action, and leave the operations of the laws to those who consider them beneficial; or to remove to another region. Here is another fallacy: even hypothetically it is not true. Each man derives his right of judgment and self-protection, not from his associated fellow-men, but from his Creator; and is by nature entitled to determine for himself, what are his rights, and to protect them, as independently of others in the community, as they are for themselves: if he submits to the adjudication and protection of government, it is because that government has taken away from him the power of exercising these rights for himself: he yields merely to power which he cannot resist; and no inference can be drawn, that he does it voluntarily. Practically the proposition is still more untrue. The individual is compelled to pay the taxes and submit to the laws of government, however unjust he may deem them: the protection given is oppressive and imperfect. As to removal to another country—the citizen's right of residence in the land where he was born, as also of a portion of its territory, is the gift of God, and not of men: and where, then, is the right of other men to impose on him the alternative of submission to laws to which he does not assent, or to depart to another country, where he has no right of residence, and where he would meet equal if not greater oppressions? The doctrine of government founded on a consent of the governed, being evinced by unavoidable acquiescence in it, is erroneous and absurd, as is every principle of right assumed for it: neither its assumptions or regulations are any where conformed to the principles of the Revolution.

Has the entire departure from these principles been inevitable? It cannot be admitted that principles almost self-evidently just and true, in plain accordance with the instructions of divine wisdom, and as plainly conducive to human elevation and felicity, are incapable of being carried into practical operation. So far from this, we believe that not only most of the evils, but also the difficulties and perplexities of civil government arise from disregard of them. It is because these "inalienable rights" are alienated to rulers, that power everywhere predominates over justice. It is because the right of "life" is disrespected, that multitudes are compelled to exposure to martial destruction. It is because the right of "liberty" is so limited, that the constraint of laws and "the rod of the oppressor" is so keenly felt, and the dark cloud of slavery obscures one half, and menaces the other half of our land. It is because "the pursuit of happiness" is not fully allowed to men, at their own discretion, but constantly regulated by the usurpations of government, that the sources of rational and elevating enjoyment are so poisoned in our social connections. Political government lays its rude, coercive hand on the most refined and most sacred of human aspirations.

Whenever this inconsistency between our theoretic declarations and our actual laws is admitted, it is not only alleged to be from necessity, which we deny, but the infringement on private rights is said to be made for "public good." Here we have to deal with one of the most extraordinary fallacies of which political history gives us any account. It is one of the most striking examples of those "time-honored" maxims, not only baseless, but absurd, which yet have been held and maintained, in all ages, by the greatest minds, merely for want of definition. What is meant by "public," and what by "good," in connexion with each other? By "good," we understand the promotion of the interest, happiness, or elevation of some intelligent being: there must therefore be such a being, to be susceptible of a good. But what being is the "public?" Has such a person or thing ever been seen? Where does it exist? what is its shape or substance? The term "public," is undoubtedly convenient in political discussion, to denote supposed combinations of the majority of individuals; but certainly does not convey an idea of any real being; and consequently not any thing which is capable of any good. "Public good" is one of those hackneyed expressions, which are useful in mystifying persons, who do not care for distinct conceptions; but which vanish at the touch of intelligent definition. Unhappily, however, this phrase has a practical, perverted import, which is not thus inconceivable. In effect, it means the interest or power of the ruling or wealthier classes of society, in disregard of the rights of the vaster number of the laboring, the poor and the ignorant. Is this a calumnious observation? Let any person examine the statute books in our country, and the reports of adjudged cases, setting aside those designed to settle private interests in special transactions, and looking only at those professing or implying regulation of public concerns; see if he can find one which does not tend to promote the interests or secure the power of the ruling or the eminent, at the expense of the multitude of the depressed. Public good virtually signifies aristocracy; literally, it signifies nothing.

If such are the effects of the departure from the principles of the Revolution, reproducing the delusions and oppressions of the transatlantic world, in a minor degree, while legislating in faithful conformity to our Constitution; how much greater a stride has been made toward despotism, by the extension of law into unauthorized enactments, which legislatures — ever prone to absorb power, and encroach on private right—have made by looseness of construction; in which the judiciary — ever leaning to the side of government — have faithfully imitated and confirmed them. Much of this is seen in our State laws, but vastly more in those of the United States. Although by the Constitution, snch ample powers are granted to the general government, as to deprive the States of every vestige of sovereignty; yet the verbal restrictions of these powers are perpetually overleaped; and the approach is manifest toward consolidated tyranny; an empire in all but the name.

The practical and pertinent question will now be asked, How could this have been avoided? How could a government have been formed mainly on the basis of the revolutionary rights, with only occasional and unavoidable imperfection? It must in candor be supposed that the respected and intelligent framers of our government did not perceive how they could have effected this; or they would have done so. At the same time we cannot avoid charging them with inattention to the subject. If they had constantly reverted to the principles of the Declaration of Independence, in enacting the separate articles of the Constitution, they could not have so formed them: the inconsistency would have been too glaring. Could they have done otherwise? If they had discarded from their minds all ideas of the prerogatives of government in the past; and without any light to guide them, but the principles announced in the Declaration of Independence, could they have constructed a government mainly on this basis? This is the question; and, although premature in the mouths of those who do not admit the failure of this trial, it can be answered.

Dismissing all the fanciful authorities alleged for the institution of government — the divine right of sovereigns; the assent of the governed; compact between each individual and the whole, which was never made; combination for safety, &c., — the only origin of it in all ages and countries, in fact, has been the sword of the warrior; the only justification of it in political reasoning, is necessity. Intelligent essayists tell the whole truth, and more than the truth, when they say, that the power of government is necessary to repel foreign encroachment, and prevent unjust injury by one citizen to another. Of course these purposes cannot be effected without some infringement of the rights of some individuals; but it is obvious, that this plea of necessity, in violation of right, ought never to be allowed any further than the necessity requires. To provisions for defence and protection, the powers of government should therefore be limited: all other regulations should be refrained from, or established in conformity to the inalienable rights of freedom. Should this principle be adopted, infringement on natural right would indeed be made in a small degree; but nine tenths of the laws made by our governments, national and state, misregulating private concerns, could be dispensed with, their object be better effected in another way; and the government be as efficient as ever. Nothing can be more true than the aphorism, that "the people who are least governed are the best governed;" multiplied legislation is suicidal in a republic.

But how can private violations of right be prevented, or disputes between individuals be settled, if power for these purposes is withheld from government? As no politicians have ever yet thought of accomplishing these objects, otherwise than by the coercive action of government, such a question is to be expected, and cannot surprise us; but, taught by the instructions of Christianity, it is believed that such ends may be attained without perpetuation — in all cases — of the agency of force; and that this agency may be remitted *pari passu* with the advance and purification of society, till it shall become even unnecessary. In the present state of all human communities, corrupted as they have been by the long continued demoralization of tyranny, force, as employed by governments, is indeed necessary for the enforcement of justice; but by no means for its determination. Government should yet be allowed the power to prevent crime, even by the uncertain *ex-post facto* administration of punishment, if no better method is discerned; but not to judge of the reality of crime, or the best measures for prevention ; still less should it be allowed to convert, by statutes, into crime, acts which neither enlightened conscience nor the laws of God have so pronounced.

The determination of these points must indeed rest somewhere : here the principles of the Revolution will guide us. If the rights of men there claimed, are, as asserted, inalienable, they cannot be alienated, all at once, by delegation to governments, and in fact they never have been so delegated ; they must of course remain with individuals, and where collisions of such rights occur between different parties, the determination of them must be by the parties themselves, or their mutually appointed representatives, in each disputed case. This leads us directly to the principle of selected reference, or, as it is called, "Arbitration," and an attentive examination will show, that this principle is effectually applicable to every case of contested right that can possibly arise in a civilized community ; and the tyranny of compelled attendance of jurors and witnesses, and the perplexing and ensnaring forms of law, would by it be dispensed with. To be sure, decisions under this method would not always be uniform, but they would be more likely to be just ; and uniformity is not attained under the present usurping system. Trials in this form, also, admit of compromises, for which our laws make no provision ; and which, in many really dubious cases, are the truest judgment.

The voluminous labyrinth of law, the extent of which is in itself a great injustice, and its innumerabls evils and oppressions, which citizens of all countries feel and complain of, are owing to the unhappy mistake made by rulers and jurists, for ages, that determinations of the respective rights, and all the perplexing encounters of the social and pecuniary interests of men can be codified ; and under this impression, statutes, and —in defect of them — precedents, are piled together in a countless array of awfully repulsive restrictions. And is completion of the system attained, or in prospect ? Does not every week's record of the Courts, present new and intricate questions, and doubtful or conflicting decisions ? On the other hand, there is in every intelligent and unbiased mind, a distinct, if not intuitive, sense of the right and the wrong, in every possible question respectively, when the facts of the case in hand are fully ascertained, which cannot be generalized or reduced to a uniform rule, but will in almost all different instances be conformable to abstract or rational justice. If this is true, it shows that the most reliable security for the determination of right, is in the judgment of a plenipotent arbitration, unbound by authority, uncorrupted by antiquated prejudices, unfettered by erroneous legislation, unbiased by official station, and unperplexed by the sophistical maxims of legal training. Such tribunals would be as satisfactory as simple; and might supersede the turmoil of partisan-political legislation, except that for protection or execution; and dismiss the immense records of laws, decisions and judicial forms to their merited oblivion.

The radical injustice of the actual principles of our government have thus been pointed out, and their entire inconsistency with those of the Revolution; and it is believed that we might safely rely on the abridgment of legislation, and a constant resort to a free, plenipotent, and competent arbitration, guided only by evidence and reason, to restore the suppressed rights of citizens, and fulfil all the legitimate purposes of government. But as the establishment of this system would be a new revolution, for which our community is not yet prepared, and cannot reasonably be expected; without such fundamental change, specific reforms might be made, in conformity to the principles of the Revolution, which might gradually approach such a change. Examples of special rules, or enactments, in which these principles are plainly contravened, of which our records of legislation and judicial decisions are full, might be produced, and which might be singly and successively reversed. Allusion has already been made to the limitations of our system of suffrage; the predominance of political sway by judicial precedents; the provisions for the support of slavery; the institution of compulsory military establishments; the extension of legal authority, by forced constructions; and the interference of government with private and social concerns, for which it never could have been instituted; further mention might be made of the regal maxims, that government cannot be sued at law by citizens; that it assumes to be a party in criminal actions, thus judging its own cause; and the imposition of oaths, expressly forbidden by Christ, and accordingly a sin in those who take, those who administer, and those who enact them; with the addition of many others, perhaps less important, but still grievous: but it is deemed unnecessary. Should they be arrayed with full comment, our Christian patriots might then be asked to survey this chaotic mass of errors, which are idolized as the perfection of human wisdom; and say, whether there is here no demand for a reformation, more radical than has hitherto been attempted.

In an earlier part of this article, it was intimated that the annunciation in the Declaration of Independence, of the equal and inalienable rights of men, was premature in an age not prepared for it, and that the time may now have come, when this principle may be raised from the grave of prescriptive policy, in which it had been buried in its infancy, and its features of divine symmetry be again exposed to the view of a more intelligent age. The forward "march of mind," and the rapid transitions of policy which have since occurred in these States; the breaking up of old opinions, and the searching analysis of prevalent dogmas, even descending to the foundations of all the social connexions of men, which characterize the present age, warrant the hope, that the righteous principles of the Revolution will no longer be neglected: indeed they are already sounded by the myriad voices of the press, though their true import is yet but dimly seen. Although none may expect their speedy recognition and full adoption, yet it is well now to lay the seeds of that tree of liberty and justice, which rising in the fostering soil of political agitation, will hereafter spread its salutary branches over our extensive empire. Believing in the constant amelioration of our race, under divine tuition, no citizen need despair of the future triumph of principles, in full accordance with celestial revelation, and manifestly tending to the high exaltation, the undeviating justice, the unrestricted freedom, the unbroken peace of the world. The dogma is not credible, that man is so corrupted in nature, as to be incapable of disinterested and unbounded benevolence; and the hope may be cherished, that sentiments of Christian love may yet break through the mighty bonds of unprincipled ambition and selfish avarice, and expand their fragrance through the whole political atmosphere of the earth.

The earnest appeal is now made to our gifted statesmen, to cast from them that vain pseudo-patriotism, which will see no faults in our growing republic, to awake to its corruptions, and re-commence the reform the Declaration of Independence promised. Let this reformation be projected in earnest, and pursued with vigor, and the character of our nation may be redeemed from the general imputation of insincerity in the profession of freedom, and dishonesty in the acquisition of territory, and the pursuit of wealth. Lauded as we every where are, for intellectual ingenuity and enterprising energy, when we shall add to these attributes, the reputation of cordial champions of the universal and inalienable rights of "life, liberty, and the pursuit of happiness," we may then stand proudly forth as "a light to lighten the Gentiles," leading them to that happy consummation announced in the birth-day song of angels, and daily solicited in the prayer that the Kingdom of the universal Father may come, and his will be done on earth, as it is done in heaven.

www.ingramcontent.com/pod-product-compliance
Lightning Source LLC
LaVergne TN
LVHW011141110826
845150LV00008B/2452
* 9 7 8 1 4 1 8 1 9 3 1 8 8 *